HONEYED LIGHT

HONEYED LIGHT

EMILY BLAIR STRIBLING

Wild Rising Press

EVERGREEN, COLORADO

Editor: Judyth Hill
Book Design: Mary M. Meade
All Art: WBHoyt
Author Photo: Sherry Streeter

www.wildrisingpress.com

First Edition
ISBN 978-1-957468-48-8

for Lucia Blair Mantel

CONTENTS

1.

An Unadorned Moment 13

Late Afternoon 14

Hunting Season 15

Departure 16

Early December Walk. 17

Not Quite Spring 18

Come June 20

June Rain 21

Mountain Walk 23

Summer Tomatoes 24

Orchard House 26

Summer Hymn Sing 28

Late Summer 30

After the Storm 31

No Trace 32

2.

Lucy 37

Baptism 38

Transitions 39

What Remains. 41

The Season of Waiting 43

Prayer for a Daughter 45

Potholders 47

What We Remember 49

Family Threads 51

Sold 52

Family Ties 54

3.

Night Poet: A Sleepover with a Bronze
Barred Owl Sculpted by Rebekah Raye . . . 59

Bird 61

At What Time of Day or Night
Can You See Angels?. 62

Just Before Sunrise 63

Coyote 64

Anchored and Owned 66

Who Marked You for Divinity? 67

Wrens 69

Wesley. 70

4.

Pandemic Poems 2020–2022 75

I Just Assumed 83

Honeyed Light 84

Trust 86

A Visitation 88

Crickets 90

Harboring 92

Fading 94

Solstice 2023 96

Advent Angel 97

5.

Selling the Farm 101

Moving 103

Resizing 104

Autumn Again 106

Returning 107

After 60 108

Acknowledgments 109

1.

The physical landscape is baffling in its ability
to transcend whatever we would make of it.
It is as subtle in its expression as turns of the mind;
and yet it is still knowable.

~Barry Lopez, *Arctic Dreams*

An Unadorned Moment

The light darts across the ferns
set on either side of the glass door,
settling on the ancient wood planks
of the long table
where we eat and celebrate
family and friends.

How to give thanks for
this unadorned moment,
this room with its bowls of sea glass,
its table of wildly tangled orchids,
its pale blue walls that hold
the voices of generations.

What a gift to pause from
the reckless rush of our days,
to be astonished,
to feel awe rising up
into full-blown joy
at the sight of sunlight
on the rough-hewn boards
of an old table.

Late Afternoon

Every autumn I see
waves of leaves
pooling at the foot of
the Japanese maple draining
its branches of all their color.

The oaks have long since tossed
their acorns onto the lawn
but still cling to their crumpled
brown leaves as if unwilling,
just yet, to undress.

Every autumn I wonder
if trees feel this as loss,
or are relieved to be free
of summer's cascade of life
invading newly greened branches,
the incessant music from dawn
till dark. Do oak and maple mind
my staring as the moon coats
the bones of their gnarled naked trunks?

Every autumn I start the fire
in early evening just as
my grandmother always did.
She'd pull her big red chair close to the flames,
cock her head, light filling
creases in her face, and point
to the silhouettes of bare trees
against the setting sun.
She said she liked to think their limbs
were raised in an *Alleluia*.
It was, she declared, a harvest benediction.
Then she lay back in her chair and rested.

Hunting Season

The fog has wiped away the mountains.
The island with its ancient lighthouse
is a smoldering ghost.

Whitecaps spin seams of white,
edging the gray waves of the bay
tumbled in the urgent tug of November tides.

A few rusted leaves cling to birch and maple.
Only one tree will go into winter
adorned with sprays of pink and orange,

bright confetti that will drop
in the snow, eventually
releasing the secret code of seeds

into the silence of dark soil.
Later the radiant silver of the
autumn moon consumes the fog,

until each star shines a restless
light on the skin of the bay as the first shot
of hunting season cracks the frozen air.

A grazing deer pauses, raises her head,
sniffs and bolts. Her blazing white tail stiffens
like a sail in the dark of night.

Departure

for Joyce

Before it's too late,
watch the light
as it settles on the lake,
as it guilds the shore
casting a keepsake of twilight.

In the canoe we paddle and
scheme about meeting
after you move.
The dying leaves release
a raw breeze.

We watch a heron
struggle to lift off,
a flare of silvered blue
bobbing on stick legs.
It's the same old story—
the urgent tug of sky and earth.

In the heron's wake
our canoe heaves and yaws,
and so it will be the same
my friend
when you depart
and it will be all I can do
to steady this boat alone.

Early December Walk

We chose to take the skyless path through the woods
beneath a dome of branches and needles.

Silence blocks words from entering this dim-lit sanctuary.

The low light becomes snow-trimmed limbs of aging balsam
and fir, a shimmer of emerald moss.

Today my heart is homeless after too many dreams.

We stand at the water's edge to see what is possible and
what is not.

Ducks and a single loon float past, black and white
diamonds against the pewter sea.

We gawk, knowing this is as close as we are allowed to the
real thing.

We stop to admire red flares of dried grasses, snow-
sequined seed pods.

The wind lit a white fire of snow that burned our cheeks.

And like fools we walked on and on into that day falling
fast into darkness, celebrating feathers and stones, grasses
and moss rising in us like a gathering of stars.

Not Quite Spring

So many things are changing
I say,

green appears and disappears
snow arrives and departs,

the sun is reckless, glaring
one minute, invisible the next,

me so easily derailed by each shift
which you don't seem to notice

as you stand, arms outstretched
embracing every new arrival,

a roving cloud or a redwing blackbird,
the chitter of new buds, a single noisy crow.

Last night I watched you bask
in the full Worm moon

its pale light streaming down
the worn grooves of your bark

a thaw signaling spring
as it has all of your eighty-plus years.

Uneasy with uncertainty
I flinch at the unexpected

while you persist, trusting your roots
to the tender mercy of wind and rain.

The song sparrows are back, the wren
has returned and I heard a hummer

just above the snowdrops ringing
your bright green mossy lap

where I settle down, leaning against
your rough trunk

to know what you have to teach me about faith.

Come June

Come June,
the garden's urgent flowers
fling fragrance and color
into the warm air
as if an ordinary day
was an occasion
to celebrate.

June Rain

The farmer watches
fog-dipped green peaks
darken deeper green,
leaves drip green,
the stream overflows.

It's past blossom drop,
and branches beaded with
cold-slowed peaches shiver
under shiftless clouds
clumping and unclumping.

He has already surrendered
prayers, his lucky rabbit tail,
his favorite hat
to make the rain stop,
and now he waits,
surveying the fresh-mown hay
where it lies wet and rotting.

He finds himself idling
somewhere between
the notion of rain
as gift and grief.

It isn't until he hears the bee
and sees the rose
planted generations ago
aflame against
the old stone wall
that he claims the gift.

He releases the grief to find
its own dark night,
dreaming instead of biting
into the juicy sun,
light running down his chin.

Mountain Walk

A soft, gray June day
after a ferocious rain,
the temperature tender.
Walking up the mountain,
throngs of mist rise,
each one its own angel,
intent on merging
into this weightless freedom,
into this sea of sky.

Summer Tomatoes

The farmer hangs the small white signs
like rungs on a ladder,
one after the other,
greens, eggs, vinegar.
Mid-May he adds the one
for *lettuce and basil,*
and finally last week
the one I've been waiting for,
tomatoes,
no capitalization, just loopy
hand-painted red letters
tilting this way and that.

I pull up to the stand
and buy three just-picked
fat tomatoes,
which is when I begin to feel
the tingle on either side
of the back of my tongue
as I imagine slivers of silky red
tomatoes and basil
a drizzle of olive oil and sea salt,

all of which takes me back to
my grandparent's brick porch,
she in the white rocker,
he on the swing sofa that needs oil,
tall glasses of iced mint tea
sweating rivers running towards
the green platter of tomato sandwiches
my grandmother set on the glass table.

That was when I had no doubt
that summer would never end nor
school ever begin as long as
we camped on this island of porch
staring at the way blue meets blue
as bay and sky merge
blurring hours and days and weeks,
unlike this year, this summer
where I count time like beans,
every moment accounted for,
every day quartered,
and so I linger at the stand to savor
this memory that once again
comes tumbling into my day like
a dream that broke loose
from the stem of night.

Orchard House
for Robert

You could say it is just a moment
in a summer flooded with blue sky
and so much light we swim in it.

You lay out the fruit you grew, bread,
cheese, blue napkins, the good sharp knife,
white plates, a yellow cruet.

A breeze rattles leaves scrawled
with family secrets these ancient trees
have guarded faithfully all these years.

Which great-grandmother was it
who waited under these maples
for her Confederate husband to surrender?

Alone all that time in their carved mahogany bed
you now sleep in, she'd been waiting
and still he didn't take her then,

choosing instead to go with his men
to the official surrender of the life
they'd always known and dreamed

while planting apple trees
and hunting deer until the Blue Ridge
swallowed the last light and went black.

This house holds all their stories
resurrected from old photographs rescued
from dark drawers and cracked walls.

And now we gather at the kitchen table
threading this moment with memory and hope,
beginning a new story,

the door opened wide to the day,
that big ripe tomato you picked glowing
like a buoy marking safe passage.

Summer Hymn Sing

Rockbound Chapel, Brooklin, ME

Seven pm the candlelit chapel is full.
We are young and old,
believer and nonbeliever,
lover and loner.
No one is ever late.

Winnie slowly lowers herself
onto the old wooden bench
as always, left side, midway back.
This week she wears a necklace
of crystal ovals that catch the light,
scattering little rainbows
across the room.
Winnie says, as of this summer,
she is 96 years old.
Margaret who sits beside Winnie
is quick to add
she is younger than Winnie at 93 years old.
They've been coming to the Hymn Sings
for as long as either can remember.

Winnie picks up the hymnal and
first thing turns to Hymn 218
In the garden.
She says she memorized the words
when she was a young girl.
As June begins to play
an old stand-up piano,
Winnie hums along,

I come to the garden alone
While the dew is still on the roses ...,

her voice is quickly absorbed
by all our voices rising from the benches
around her
when all of a sudden, we
hear her crescendo
above all the others,
releasing her unending praise,
Winnie holds the last note

until the flickering
of the holy
shines in each one of us.

And the joy we share as we tarry there
None other has ever known ...

Late Summer

They flicker still,
the last fireflies,
not pulsing with desire
as in June
but still here,
unbuttoning their light
more slowly,
giving us time to savor
what's left of warm nights,
giving the crickets time
to tune up. Already
one red leaf
rests in the grass.

After the Storm

We sit on the screened-in porch,
the presence of silence like
a friend who's traveled
the way with us these twenty-plus years,
watching the storm muscle
into this sizzle of an afternoon,
bruising the sun-drenched sky
with dark thunderheads.
Bulbous white clouds edged in gold
burst and the rain begins.

I flinch when lightning rips
open the sky's skin.
It bleeds radiance.
We both feel thunder's shudder.
He reaches over, takes my hand.
This is not the first storm
we've navigated together
nor will it be the last.
The lights flicker, go out,
come back on.

After the storm a stillness
with its calm embrace of sky,
water, mountain, and us,
the wet green scent of leaves and grass.
Oh, but what a performance when
sky and earth knock heads.
We too have gone shoulder
to shoulder with fury—
we know the fierce consolation
in weathering
yet another untamed storm.

No Trace

The field out back is mowed.
Potatoes, garlic and onions cured,
pesto and tomato sauce stored,
and the last to be harvested
winter squash on its cellar shelf.
In the garden only solitary stalks
of kale and chard remain.

Tomorrow we will put away
the porch furniture,
snap in storm windows, coil hoses,
stack the last of the wood.
Hay is in the barn, the water pipe taped.
In the paddock only goldenrod
retain their color.

We have removed all traces of summer
as if we had never floated
on the smooth surface of its
pond of light, and let
time go its own way,
as if we had never lingered
to watch falling stars
dapple the shores of night,

as if we had never grilled
fresh cod,
as if the fading light hadn't haloed
our visiting children,
telling each other the stories
of their grownup lives,
as if we had never played croquet
or sailed past Pumpkin Light.

Like a dream we don't remember,
summer slips away from us,
pale filaments swirling
in the gold-flecked air of autumn,
only the eternity of sea and sky,
the final blue burst
of hydrangea.

2.

There are only two lasting gifts we can give our
     children.
One is roots, the other wings.

~ Wise Woman

Lucy

You were handed to me
at 3 days old, asleep mostly, except
for that glassy cry that pierced our hearts,
father, mother, two grandmothers, grandfather,
all of us wounded by your need
until you latched onto your mother,
the warm milk making its way,
into every chamber of your tiny body.

Now you eat Goldfish and mango,
black beans and organic avocado,
you love dogs and balls but not bows.
Your little feet smack the wooden floor
in rhythm with a music we don't hear,
and you talk words, non-words,
lost words, all together lift and twirl
glittering in the sunlit air,
molecules bonded to hope.

That first time I heard you say my name
you laughed,
looking around as if you saw
the generations of women who came before,
all gathered right there around us
to welcome your becoming,
to make sure you know
your parents are the bones,
your grandparents the marrow.

Baptism

We drive home to the farm after the baptism.
The newest cousin fed and blessed to sleep,
the older children play by the fire.
It is late afternoon and the rain comes
like an afterthought for our thanksgiving
for the gift of water.

There are no grapes on the vine.
The hay is in and rests like huge spools of twine,
row after row along the fence line.
Already cows graze the stubble of bare fields
that stretch like an ochre skin all the way
to distant mountains.

We watch the last few geese fly over,
their cries pierce a wind strong enough
to snap a jagged branch.
We hurry to the house
to kindle the first fire of the season.
Lest we forget, the story of light
is the beginning of it all.

Transitions

for Alexander

Flecked brown and white feathers
fluffed out around the chest
catch my eye first,
then I see the rust-tipped tail
and curled yellow claws,
gripping nothing more than
the memory of a branch,
one gleaming amber eye
and a beak hooked
into its own dark descent.

I pause on the concrete steps
of the school's science building
where the bird lies on its side.
I know it is a red-tailed hawk
just like the one we used to watch
in the meadow behind the barn
riding the drafts, dipping
its wings into one windy wave
after the other, feathers
dripping with light.

You were seven then, reed thin
and as blonde as winter wheat
and every day after feeding the sheep,
you'd make me watch
as you climbed the ladder
to the hayloft,
took hold of the knotted rope
and swooped, like the hawk,
for one brief moment
above it all.

The day the hawk disappeared
you wanted to know why.
I said I couldn't tell you
and you kicked the ground
and refused to move
until I gave you the reason.
And I began to weigh
reason against the death of hope
while the dust you kicked up
settled around us like a cloud.

You're fourteen now, wiry
and strong as a young tree.
Your hair is darker,
but I still see the wisps
of wheat glinting in the sun.
We squeeze into the doorway
of your new room with
its orange rug and two windows
looking out at the ancient red brick
schoolhouse, the chapel, library
and gym.

There's not enough room
for the two of us here.
It's time I leave you
to claim the questions and
answers on your own,
to sift through sorrows
and joys, to risk becoming
all you can be. Go, my boy, go
learn to love what is
for its own sake.

What Remains

At the airfield I waited with you
for the plane that will carry you back
to the city where you turn the pages of
your life and new stories begin,
where sidewalks run like rivers
into light-streaked dreams.
And there is so much time.

Here on this peninsula in Maine
where I have come to live we are
more water than mountain
more sky than earth
and my time recovered
from its crimped schedule
now drifts free as a feather
in salt-soaked air.

There are more pine trees here,
but the snow is the same powdery
newborn white, the light the same pink gold
as it was when we used to sled
down the hill at the farm,
you sewn to my back,
your arms roped around my neck.

In the Berkshires
where you grew up sailing the pond,
a Navy Seal steering a striped raft,
bravely navigating around suspected
water snakes and toads,
you collected fireflies
for night vision.

In New York and Washington,
you sipped red wine and
ate shrimp and truffle tapas,
this time searching for
how to navigate around jobs
and serious girlfriends,
all to find one thread

to reconnect you to the farm,
where you believed you could
be a Navy Seal one day and
hit home runs the next,
where you unwrapped every day
to discover what new charm
lay in the palm of your hand.

When you waved from the plane,
a swirling scrim of snow between us,
I saw your eyes exploring mine,
searching for any traces
of the way back to the farm
and its fences that contained

the sure shape of your world.
Instead, what you find is an
island of love. Today the wind
tangles trees, the house shakes and
sea smoke rises. From my window
the ocean surges and retreats—
only its islands remain the same.

The Season of Waiting

I was thinking how you used to
nest in my lap, a knot of overalls
and blonde hair, a cheek
in the crook of my arm, the wings
of your dreams lifting off.

It made me smile but not wish to go
back to when you were young.
I like who you have become,
the way your mind prowls the
streets of new ideas,

the way your heart approaches
pain and kindness with
the same determination
to mine the light that flows
deep in your bones.

But in the dimming of December
when I hang the wreaths and play
the old Paul Winter concerts,
when I pick holly and hum the
Advent hymns, it begins,

the swarm of bright memories.
I become a hive of the past,
housing all those years it took
you to build the strong walls
of who you are.

Then comes the moment when
poetry and metaphor are not enough,

when memories make the mind sticky,
when I can no longer see your
reflection in the well of night.

I want to find your one wool sock
in the dryer, the dishes in the sink,
the pile of books by your chair.
I want to see the puddle of water
from your boots on the floor,

I want to hear you call Mom
as if you believed I could still calm
your fears, and I want
to answer you as if I still believed
I could offer you a harbor.

As we move towards Solstice,
toward that moment
when the needle of light drips
slowly into the earth's veins,
restoring a pulse of hope,

I will take the hand each day
offers, inhale balsam and
seek the advice of stars.
I will trace flakes of snow and
follow the wake of eiders,

until in jeans and blue parka
you walk across the runway
and memory and hope begin
to dance on a shining floor
flinging light into the night.

Prayer for a Daughter

For Sara

The sun doesn't lie.
It takes the same path across the sky
every year. I know it is September.
I sweep the dying leaves
red, yellow, lavender
off the granite stairs
up to the porch
where we gathered
all summer
a family of three
to feast on the love,
trust and laughter
we took years to get right.

Sunday nights
you drove the black truck
to the Mexican takeout
and brought home quesadillas
oozing cheese and crab
and together we watched
as the sun swathed
the lighthouse in
ribbons of pink
and the moon
like a pale lily
pressed through the
soil of night.

Now on this Sunday night
as the sun settles
into the arms of trees,

worn out from
flinging hazy gold
at chilly winds,
the porch is dark,
a lone buoy tolls.
I light a candle
and the two of us
left behind
talk about what you
might be doing at this hour.

What time is it in Dakar?
You, whose smile in the photo does not lie,
you who collects light
to share with others,
you who can convince
flowers to bloom,
and biscuits to rise,
you who can milk goats
and play the piano,
are the gift gathering voice
and tone and rhythm
while we, like the sun,
take the same path into winter.

Potholders

for Sara

When she visits, she notices everything.
If I've moved the tea bags or repotted
the geranium, or replaced a doorknob,
such insignificant pieces of a life she
left years ago, after college.

She has traveled the world, walked the
Great Wall of China, swum with
sharks in Cape Town, visited
the Taj Mahal in India, treated herself
to street corner crêpes in Paris.

She has stayed in hostels and hovels,
helped farmers grow tomatoes, took
time to raise a goat, learned Wolof,
returning only when she completed her
Peace Corps tour in Senegal.

She tells me she dreams of the sun
setting over Kilimanjaro, gold and jewel
encrusted saris of India, the cold blue
of the ocean on the coast of Normandy,
the blue and yellow Portuguese azulejos.

Yet she returns year after year
to the blue mountains and clear lakes
in the town where we still live,
our windows awash with light
that fades the fabric of our days.

Last time she handed me two
quilted potholders, each printed with a small
bird on a flowering branch. She knows
I love birds. She says she imagines
each bird has a story, and we laugh

as I stir the soup, she fills the bowls.
I say a silent prayer of thanksgiving
for a daughter who is so finely tuned
to what matters.

What We Remember

You said you remembered
we didn't have much money
when you were growing up.

I remember
we had enough
for your baseball cards
and your Iceys—
you always chose cherry,
coming home with a big
red stain of a mustache.

You said you remembered
you wore your cap brim backwards,
your black backpack
bulging with books.

I remember
your blue eyes
scouring every
moment for what
it might offer that was
new and shiny and bold.

You said you remembered
running down the court,
the ball spinning off
your hands into the net.

I remember
how after a big snow
the city blanketed

in such a pure silence,
we walked the dog
in the dark,
right up the middle
of Park Avenue.

Is it always the way
with mothers and sons,
that she has forgotten
the notes and he the song?

But the music
is still there,
drifting through
their days, sometimes
loud, sometimes not.
They both hear it,
mother and son.

Family Threads

It is extravagant, I know,
the big vase of blue hydrangea and lavender phlox
for just the two of us.

All summer this house has been full of children,
the fragrance of small voices wafting through its rooms,
seashells and painted rocks, small tokens of wonder.

We gathered as one family,
three generations from two to seventy-two,
all pulling up chairs to the old table,

all talking at once, all hungry to be fed,
sometimes accepting, other times rejecting
all that we are and we aren't.

We make no more, no less, of how children and grandchildren
refuse to let us help them tie their shoes,
or build a castle or find a job.

For these few weeks we return to where it all began,
the fireflies, the picnics, swimming,
wine on the porch, lobsters and peach pie,

shooting stars that from birth
lured this family back to do it all again and again.
Now it is just the two of us here in the old farmhouse,

caretaking memories as a new season begins
to tell a new story about the blessing of seeds
and dying leaves the wind whips and swirls.

We light the fire, pour the wine,
a prayer lodging between us
for the return of the prodigal light.

Sold

Swan's Island

This is the island
where we watched the whales.
My grandmother, holding my hand,
hooted with joy as
a great blue hulk
launched itself into the air
and splashed wildly down.

This is the island
where we climbed the old stone wall
to follow the path to the sea,
to swim in the heart-stopping
Maine water, the stony beach
warm under our feet.

This is the island
where every August
the family gathered on the porch
to celebrate my mother's birthday
gorging on lobsters, fresh corn
and chocolate cake. Always
afterwards, our parents napped.

This is the island
where I had thought my children
would bring their children
to watch the whales.
But they married and scattered,
moved to cities and
watch movies instead.

This is the island
where I came to accept
a house needs voices and
laughter, poems and stories,
waking and sleeping,
not absence and stillness,
not light dying in the corner.

This is the island
where today I stare at
black-and-white photos
taken before I was born,
of the house and old barn.
Tomorrow, I will send them
to the new owner.

Family Ties

We, who stagger under the weight
of all that we have accumulated—
degrees, jobs, houses, children,
husbands, wives, songs and stories,
silverware, cake pans and plates
we once imagined we would
be handing on to our children—
now wonder where to lay them down.

We had expected our children
might've wanted to collect
the family stories,
like the one about their great-aunt
who hoarded colored beach glass,
wore grey overalls to every occasion,
preferred vodka neat and
never married. Or the one

about the grandmother who
recorded birdsong and night owls
in her nightgown until the neighbors
complained and called the police.
Maybe they would want to know
their great-uncle received
a medal for valor in WWII
when he entered an enemy town in Germany
alone whistling "Oh Shenandoah"
to make sure his troops would be safe.

In the past all these stories mattered.
They were told and retold.
Family repeated itself,

adding yet another story,
another cake pan, another song
as proof they belonged.
Instead, they trust a button
to give them instant family.
Meanwhile I try to have faith that
like the trees, our children
will be sustained through
a system of roots we do not see,
passing along what it takes
for families to stay connected,
to teach their children our songs.

3.

Until one has loved an animal, a part of one's soul remains unawakened.

~Anatole France

Night Poet: A Sleepover with a Bronze Barred Owl Sculpted by Rebekah Raye

In my arms,
the bronze weight of you
is cold and impervious.
It is only when I hold
your sweet head
in my hands and my thumbs,
trace around your eyes
and your bent-over beak,
that you nest in my heart.

I stare into those
unfathomable eyes,
all pitch-black compassion.
The sun streaks layers of
coppery bronze feathers.
It is the v of your talons
that steadies you.
The words that emerge
belong to both of us.

After the silence of winter's
snow and sleep,
that hush of all creatures,
the racket of spring begins,
the sweat and promise
of day overtaking night,
the clatter of leaves
big as plates,
and the invisible symphony
of bird and beast
jams the airwaves.

You know enough to wait
for the ebb of day's noisy debris
before you beam
your longings into darkness—
Who cooks for you,
Who cooks for you
you repeat over and over
until even the stillness vibrates
with such insistent desire.

Night after night,
from where you perch
in the cavity of the rotting oak
at the edge of the woods,
you call and wait.
Night after night
you scribble your dreams,
small poems on the backs of stars.

Finally, one night
an answer.
After a rush of high-pitched
caws and hoots and gurgles
she joins you, squeezing
herself in beside you,
and soon in a flurry of
brown and grey feathers,
a new life begins to churn.

And I must confess I envy
your faith in what
you couldn't see but dared to love
just the same.

Bird

That such a small word
could contain so many feathers
and songs, and all that down,
white and grey dreamed-of softness,
not to mention
legs, and beaks and eyes,
nestled like tiny jewels
among the fluff.

Then there are those little hearts,
keeping time for all those songs
that will cross oceans,
light on mountaintops,
sweeten the lives of lonely stars,
only to return home
to nest in one small word.

At What Time of Day or Night
Can You See Angels?

I usually don't see them but my cat does.
Early mornings, just before dawn
he springs up onto the table
where I catch him staring out the window,
his ears pricked, his long, stripy
tail swishing back and forth.
I inspect the lawn carefully. Nothing.
My eyes search the woods. Nothing.
I notice his shoulders begin to quiver as if
he was preparing to pounce. On what?
I look again. Nothing. He doesn't pounce.
Instead he pirouettes off the table
and races back and forth behind the couch,
a tornado of joy,
up the stairs, down the stairs.
Rattling the enamel charger,
he nearly knocks the lamp off the table
as he settles himself on the sofa,
paws stretched out, eyes closing,
head bowing as in prayer.
What he saw made him leap
and dance and his eyes ...
oh, his eyes were so light-filled
that only an angel could have lit them.
Oh brave-hearted cat,
you find what is there
while I go looking.

Just Before Sunrise

I walk the dog this morning
just before sunrise.
Leftover light
from stars and moon
glimmers on mounds
of frozen snow.

I see diamonds.
The dog sees hoofprints.
I inhale the fresh breath
of the newborn day.
The dog inhales the scent
of deer and rabbit
and wags his tail.

On such an ordinary day,
we stand in the meadow
watching the sun rise,
until the glare fuses
the distance between
diamonds and hoofprints.

I wonder how much more
perfect one moment can be
than this one
when we are allowed
to find our own way
into the pocket of joy
together.

Coyote

It is different every night,
the way the moon lies
on the water. Sometimes
it freezes like a silver skin,
covering the bay.
Other times it flickers,
romps in the waves.

I know because I am awake,
standing at the black
mirror of window,
overlooking the bay,
which is when I see the
silhouette of the coyote
on our stone wall and

hear its piercing howl.
The dread rises in me.
I begin to account for
chickens and goats,
dog and cat,
son and daughter,
husband and me.

The coyote stretches,
noses the air and
leaps off the wall,
vanishing like a dream,
details smudged
by the bleary darkness.

From behind a cloud
the moon slips and haws,
maneuvering between stars,
its shine weaving bay
into land, tree into
sky and me into
a holy silence.

Anchored and Owned

The panic always waits until
the middle of the night,
wrenching me out of flowery dreams,
spinning my heart like a dreidel,

and I go straight into my list
of what is undone and fixate
on the propane I forgot to order,
how cold the house will become,

what if the bear breaks down
the door again to get at the garbage
in the garage or the squirrel nesting
in the wall dies,

why won't my stomach digest
dinner without making me feel
as if there is a dance party
stomping under my ribs,

and why does my mind orbit
the dark spitting sparks of shame
that I left the dinner dishes
unwashed in the sink?

It isn't until the dog curls up
beside me, his head on my chest,
that I settle into the night,
anchored and owned.

Who Marked You for Divinity?

No one I know of,
but I like wondering
what it would feel like
if the sky opened up
and a dove,
or maybe even a robin,
flew down and God spoke.

Would I laugh nervously,
startled at all the fuss,
or would I run for my life
at being tagged?

That gray day at the Jordan,
soggy from being dunked
in the murky water,
Jesus looked up as words
about sonship tumbled down
from the clouds.
There was nothing about
a daughter.

The fact remains,
only God could've come up with
iridescent pink blended into
the gray feathers of the dove,
which is to say it is clear
she is already marked
by divinity and knows
whereof she sings.

As I sit here watching my feeders,
the red cardinal, goldfinch,
chickadees, the rowdy blue jays,
I confess I do not need
the sky to open,
but I do listen,
in case one of these creatures
might call me beloved.

Wrens

All morning
I watched the wrens,
male and female,
fly between the wisteria
and an old oak,
not thinking about
pollution or forgiveness,
fossil fuel or injustice.
No squawking,
no calling back and forth,
no silky hum of feathers.

They are freehearted
with each other,
taking turns,
transferring one
tiny twig at a time,
bits of moss
and puffs of dried grass
from beak
to the bird house.
They aren't distracted
by me or the dog or
the bluebird who
nosedives them
for property rights.

I marvel at their diligence,
being so precisely
who they are called to be,
to eat, to build,
to birth, to sleep
and always to sing.

Wesley

By this time, I should know
you are not there.
But my foot continues to feel
for the length of you
asleep beside the bed,
the sun rising over your black back,
spilling onto the floor,
the thump of your white-tipped tail telling me
it's time. As always you wait for me
so we can take this day together.

After chores, the barn door closed,
the sun setting on our way home
and darkness shouldering in,
you trot beside me, your work done,
as always the day met so wholeheartedly,
so abundantly as if it might be your last
until it was.

That day we had walked on the beach,
you swam, chased a stick and then collapsed,
every cell in your body suddenly shredded
by the blast of the infection
buried deep in your marrow.
At the hospital
you placed your paw on my hand,
as if you knew it was time
for me to let go.

The months pass and it is autumn—
a rainbow of leaves flutters
against an enamel blue sky.

I button my jacket and set out
into this new season alone.
I am trying to understand
how to hold your absence
as dearly as you held my presence.

4.

Faith is the bird that feels the light and sings when
the dawn is still dark.

~Tagore

Pandemic Poems 2020–2022

1.

Out of an abundance of caution
I pray often and don't hesitate to beg.

Out of an abundance of caution
I use up all the soap in the house.

Out of an abundance of caution
I have enough wine to last.

Out of an abundance of caution
I do not cry so anyone can hear me.

Out of an abundance of caution
I buy my husband 18 cans of Dr. Pepper.

Out of an abundance of caution
I count tissues in the wastebasket.

Out of an abundance of caution
I tap the sunrise for its sweetness.

Out of an abundance of caution
I check the North Star every night.

Out of an abundance of caution
I carried 12 salamanders off the road.

Out of an abundance of caution
I plant peas and hope.

Watching for what we cannot see
will eventually damage
what we can see.
I say be careful that in detouring
around the ordinary flow of grace
we do not miss the gifts
any given spring day has to offer,
flower and leaf, hawk and heron, sun and rain
and the fragrance of warm, newborn air.

2.

My phone chimed and
up came the notification:
"No *upcoming events, reminders or alarms,*"
as if I didn't already know that.

This morning, lying in bed,
I am trying to recall
what day it is because
at the very least,
it tags time as particular,
and when I finally come up
with Wednesday because
NBC news mentioned that
yesterday was the Tuesday
before Easter,
I get up and dress,
determined once again to devise
a new way into another day.

It isn't until late in the afternoon
that I begin to wonder how
we will remember
the hours and days and weeks and months

of our quarantine,
our social distancing,
our sheltering in place,
our lockdown,
our stay at home,
our isolation
as more than
one blank day stacked
on top of another.

The nights are more manageable.
The quiet that settles into
the mountains belongs here.
The moon waxing and waning
is dependable, light
comes and goes on time.
The deer stomping
in the woods,
the solitary bobcat
padding its way across the lawn,
the wings of the heron
thumping a way to the pond
begin to make order of the hours.
I release my own story
and in this ease finally I sleep.

3.

I pull the elastic over one ear and then the other,
I resettle the mask over my nose and mouth
before entering the food store and trying to breathe.

They say to move quickly and not to linger.
I buy a small head of cabbage, white balsamic vinegar,
ginger, milk, cashews, pay and leave.

I have my own Clorox wipes. The handle of
the cart, my hands, the steering wheel are
all toweled off before I start the car.

The dog gives me a look I don't understand
until I realize I still have my mask on. I tell
him I am who he thinks I am.

At the package store I run into the owner who admires
the print on my mask. I tell her my friend, Sue, made
it for me. She tells me Sue made hers also.

Hers a pink abstract print, mine a pale blue paisley pattern
cover our smiles and mute our gratefulness,
hide our compassion and camouflage our fear.

On the drive home I wonder how to make sense
of comparing masks instead of asking after our children
or sharing a good book or news of a friend?

Self-protection comes at a such a high premium. It demands
we wear a disguise to keep us safe. Even the dog knows.
I only hope our prayers can escape our masks.

4.

We have been quarantined now
for 58 days and 58 nights.
My prayer at first was simple.
     O God, *please keep our children and us safe.*
No histrionics, no begging, no bargaining.
Stay at home and stay safe.
We can do that.
Somewhere around day 41
things began to change.

Time had lost its color.
Days and nights have no margins.
I see images of my children on screens
I cannot hug. I see images of my friends
on screens, their blank eyes reflecting mine.

Dreams I have them. They have me.
One night I kept resewing the blue
and green print squares that
wouldn't stay put on the quilt.
Another night I transplanted roses
that wouldn't stay where I planted them.
Still another I spent restringing beads because
they kept slipping off the wire onto the floor.
Tears backed up on me.
My prayer got more complicated.
       O God, *I have come this far, learned to loosen my love*
and replace my anger, learned the names of stars,
learned to trust the light of the moon, learned to listen to
 the conversation of trees without interrupting, learned to
release my children to enter their own stories
and my husband to his own. Please, please do not let me
lose the person I've become.
What I haven't learned yet is how to hold enough space for
       our grief.

5.

Every day at 5:30 I call my friend Pam.
Every day. We don't skip.

One evening the phone call was about the bear
who scratched and pawed her back door open,

and then without spilling, lifted the whole can

of bird seed out onto the terrace and gorged.

A day after that Pam called to say the bear
made a second visit, tearing the door off its hinges.

He left grouchy because there was no food.
She said she didn't want to share her kitchen with the bear.

I agreed but wondered if we had made a mistake
calling the bear *he* when in fact it was a *she*?

Pam said she didn't care if it was a he or a she,
she still didn't want the bear in her house.

Some days all we have to say to each other
is small potatoes: music, tea bags, weather,

the red fox that crossed by her pond, the red-tailed
hawk that lives in our woods, masks vs scarves.

It doesn't matter what we talk about, only
there is a point in every day when we pause

to be reminded of the friendship that
has fastened our lives together all these years,

will hold the space for our grief and laughter,
our anger and joy until no day passes unnoticed.

6.
            for WMB

It is a small painting, its frame
is wood stained silver.
It is not one of your seascapes

that covers a whole wall with wind
and waves that have me tasting salt,

and it is not one of your landscapes
harnessing wild green meadows and
mountains that offer up the music
of streams and the sweet grassy breath
of grazing cows.

When I first saw this painting
I found I was unable to ignore
the fully opened begonias bursting
pink and peach and orange massed
in the blue-grey porcelain vase,

and I couldn't help but notice
the shine on the spring onions
or how the glass candlesticks
with their square green candles
claimed a space of their own.

As if that wasn't enough, there was
the sweep of indigo blue background
that turns those ordinary items
on the fertile field of your canvas
into stars of their own universe.

It hangs on the wall just above
where we gather to eat and speak
our way into one more day
emptied of family and friends,
errands and events,

and yet its flare of color always
gives us opulent hope and deep

gratitude for the sheer pleasure
these objects take in simply
being together on a table.

I Just Assumed

I just assumed that I'd always know
that safety, like love, was as given as gravity,
that if I made my bed I could trust
there were angels watching over me,
as that's what the prayers I recited
every night reassured me.

There would always be a barn
where, morning and evening,
I'd climb a wooden ladder
into the warm loft; inhale
the bales of sweet dried grasses
before opening them to feed
the animals waiting below.

I just assumed there would always be
Angus cattle inking the front fields,
pigs and chickens around back,
horses, all six of them, turned out
in the side field where the stream ran
like a dark vein, edging the woods
into the heart of the farm.

I never expected to lose it all.
The family, the farm, the childhood angels.
Town houses have replaced the cows.
The barn made into an edgy condo.
Family like the angels all flown.
I no longer despair of the past.
I've learned to navigate a passage
between memory and hope and
allow wonder to take the wheel.

Honeyed Light

My mother and I sit on the terrace
this early autumn afternoon
and reminisce about old friends
whose names have worn
through her memory
like fingers in an
old pair of gloves.

In the distance
mountains rise and fall,
blue waves in a sea of sky.
A golden light
thick as honey
runs down their craggy sides.
My mother sees an ocean
and asks about the ships
on the horizon.

I see the bee when it lands
on her wrist and hear
my mother's parched skin
crack under the bee's
feathered black velvet feet.
There is no sting,
only the gentle flutter
of wings,
and the bee is gone.

I want to ask her if she believes
God sends angels disguised
as bees when I see
she has fallen asleep,

as ships, waves, daughter
fade into the honeyed light
and details float like motes
on her dreams.

Trust

I help you on with your coat.
One sleeve at a time,
I pull the navy blue Melton
over the arc of your spine.
You are bent now,
poised like a diver
on the high board,
one step and you might
find yourself hurling
head over heels
into the unforgiving
deep end.

I wonder how it looks from
where you are,
and how long we have
until you release your grip
and go
where, Mother, where?

You take my arm as
we make our way out
into the cool November morning
to stroll the dirt road.
The sun inflames the oak
until it glows like a torch.
You say it turned gold
from dying weeks ago.
How can you talk about death
shining, Mother, shining?

You tell me you want
to go home
and as we turn back,
I hear each breath you take
barely squeezing through
the dark, crumbling
passageway of your lungs.
Pausing, you look up
at the cloudless sky
as if surely you see
a heaven
in the sweep of lucent blue.

And in all that expectant joy,
you let go
and I catch you,
as if we'd been practicing
our whole life.

Now fitted against me
the way I once fitted
against you,
trust me, Mother, trust me
as I once trusted you.
I will not let go.

A Visitation

This is the second night in a row
I dream about my mother,
her blonde hair curled at her shoulder
her eyes not so much sky as sapphire.
She is wearing her straight black skirt
and white blouse, collar up,
a pink cashmere sweater thrown
over her narrow shoulders.

One hand twists
the gold chain she always wore,
the other she tucks against her hip
like a small wing.
She is watching all of us, family and friends
who find themselves present,
just as they always had been present
at the farm where we grew up.

Our home collected friends
as if we were the local shelter
where people came to drop off
their relatives they could
no longer keep.
My mother took them all in,
my friends, my brothers' friends,
friends of friends.
She listened to their stories,
and received their dreams
as tokens of hope.

And then she is gone,
vanishing into a swell of light.

Not once—twice. Two nights
of my believing that soon
we would be gathering
at the table set with the silver candlesticks,
the ruby glint of her wineglass
flashing,
the voices of friends and family
drawling into the dawn.

The night she died
the undertaker unhooked
the gold chain from around her neck
and handed it to me.
I keep it in my drawer along
with her white gloves.
I wear her wedding ring
alongside mine.

Crickets

It is late August and I open the door
to the night and its sounds,
the shrieking howl of coyote,
a rabbit slipping through the grass,
the drawl of waves on the shore,
the crickets beginning to crescendo.
And I hear my mother's voice,
"Six weeks to the first frost."

On warm, jasmine-scented summer nights,
as my mother sat out on her terrace
sipping her last glass of wine
and staring out at the blue shadows
of distant mountains,
she listened to the night
begin the story of tomorrow.
She said she felt
it entitled her to hope.

Even as she lay dying,
she begged us to open the window
so she could hear what the night
had to tell her about
how it all doesn't end.
There is more to the story.
Even as the crickets sing
themselves out of this life,
there will be a new season

blazing with presence,
rubbing its silky wings together,
intent on making its own kind of music,

just as these crickets do tonight.
I wish my mother back
to assure me of what lies ahead.

Harboring

For RMS

You're right the phone doesn't ring
like it used to, and a full night's sleep
is as elusive as winning the lottery.
There is no question you could
use a dose of sun instead of another
gray January day, but honestly
when you saw that red siren of
a cardinal at the feeder this morning
didn't you feel delight.

While there are more doctors'
appointments, your fussy heart
wants your attention, and all those
greedy tests that consume hours
of your time, you still walk miles
every day, still shovel the snow,
still carry the wood. Yes, we
are older now, the body is softer,
the mind is deeper.

It is all holy, the way one day
unfolds into the next. The surprise
of what we don't expect is still there.
The mystery of leaf and flower
appearing, disappearing,
only to appear again, the flutter of
clouds, the fragrance of lilac and lily,
the pursuit of dog and squirrel, the taste
of the first snowflake on your tongue.

Listen to me, you have to hang in there,
if only to recall that late August day

at the end of the season when
we entered the harbor, sail stiff,
boat heeled from a warm wind
muscling down the Reach
when we caught our mooring
in one pass, locked the tiller
and settled back to watch the sun set,
the dog and you and me
glowing gold as the water.

Fading

Every day, I mean every day including Sunday,
my friend wrote her to-do lists:
Put in a wash
Write birthday card
Exercise
Bead new necklace
Volunteer Food Bank
Buy wine and tomatoes for dinner.

Scratching out each task
as it was accomplished,
she would begin a new list
for the next day.
I envied her ability to organize her life,
hours, days, weeks in advance.

Today we sit together,
sipping tea steaming
into the safety of silence
when suddenly she asks
why are there glass chickens
on the shelf next to my shower?

Did you notice how the light
turns the blue glass hens
aquamarine,
purple ones to amethyst?
Then she withdraws,
her words fading into
late afternoon light.
I imagine I once
might have been on her list
as *Tea at 4pm.*

Now there are no more lists,
her mind has set free familiar names.
Hours have lost their way from
the clock to where she sits trying
to reshape time, ordering clothes
she will never wear, chocolate
she will never eat. Her writing
takes off across the page
like a flock of birds into the horizon.
Only she can see it.

Solstice 2023

Yes, I know it is dark,
but hold us here a little longer
in the stillness,
that the glitter and glare
do not distract us from
learning to trust there is
more,
go deeper into the silence
where we find dark's consolation,

like the way grass whispers
to our feet as its roots stretch
and flutter,
or the way stars flower the sky,
petals of light
blossoming in our eyes,
or the way we hear the ocean
humming,
wave after wave,
its lullaby to the shore.

On this last night before the solstice
as we wait for the brightness,
let us linger in the dark
long enough to receive its gifts,
intertwining threads
of who we are with more,
and reminding us,
we cannot see the light
without the darkness.

Advent Angel

Her name is Willa.
She is taller than I am.
She loves candles,
ones that smell like fir trees
and ones that smell like roses.
She likes to wear forest green
and magenta together,
and old brown boots.
She wore them in the stable
when she visited the baby.
She told me she remembers
the sweet scent of hay and hide,
the steady chomping of
the animals gathered round
that rickety manger,
as if there was nothing
special about God
being born bona fide
blood and bone snuggled
in the straw to keep warm,
which is when she saw streams of light
flow into the barn and into
every cranny in her body.
She said she comes
to bring that light
to help us find a way through
this season of silence,
the dark waiting of
the hoped-for unknown.

5.

We must let go of the life we planned, so as to accept the one that is waiting for us.

~Joseph Campbell

Selling the Farm

It came slowly to us,
like the ending of a love affair
we didn't want to let happen.
It was time to sell the farm.
Here's the love affair part:
my goats and chickens at home
in the most grand and beautiful
red barn in whose solid walls
were embedded the spirits
going back years of all
the livestock it had housed.

Then there was the blast
of gold light as the sun rose
over the bay that began our day,
the lilacs sweetening the air in June
only to give way to the fragrance
of pine and spruce burning
in the woodstove in December.
How the land fed and shaped us.
Its extravagant claims
on our time and energy
willingly surrendered
until now.

But the land has also schooled
us about how hard it is to
transplant roots.
We did not grow up by the ocean.
We were born at the foot
of blue mountains and clear streams.
It was not the sound of waves

and whispering evergreens
that lulled us to sleep
but the soft chorus of sycamore
and oak that plays in us to this day.

Moving

My friend says he is moving and
in me a furnace of feelings heats up.
The trips to Goodwill with
books and plates and heavy sweaters,
the plants handed over to friends,
the black trash bags full of old files
and faded albums.
The past now in a landfill
the future in boxes.
The heartbreak of taking apart
a home,
a delicate ache.

Resizing

I made a list of what we couldn't take:

My grandmother's chest of drawers,
the green braided rug in the dining room,
the two beds upstairs,
the 25 long-stemmed wineglasses,
the yellow plates I got at a tag sale,
the books, two hundred books, that went to the
    library sale,
the red geraniums I've watered for 9 years,
the sheets and towels that went to the homeless shelter.
A son took my mother's table lamps,
the sailboat was sold, the old Corvette given away.

It is late spring, the air still cool,
the bay deepening blue, the lilacs
budded up tight.
The farm has been bought,
the goats and chickens rehomed.
I clean out the birdhouses
and gather the last of the marigold
seeds from the greenhouse.
I stand in my garden, the garlic
thrusting its silky stalks through straw
I had spread to protect them
from the cold. Another year I would've
had my peas and lettuce already in
the ground.

Someone asked if we were downsizing,
I said we are resizing, paring down,
pare coming from the Latin to prepare,

to prepare for what is ahead or
to prepare for where it all began,
not on this ocean peninsula but
on a farm. Both of us born
landlocked, we were taught
how to bring in the cows,
learned how to recognize
weather riding in clouds.
We are older but not old yet.
We still look forward
to night skies strewn with stars,

the vast silence of mountains
and clear lakes protected
by herons and hawks.

The last of the boxes packed,
what we leave behind can't be
contained in a heart or a poem.

Autumn Again

Pinned on the refrigerator is the photo,
the three of us at our college graduation
just before we headed, pitching and yawing,
into marriages and children, divorces,
remarriages, jobs and no jobs.
The mystery of what comes after
as distant as the silver bubble of moon
floating in the dark of space.

We are friends who have threaded
our way, indelible and constant,
through the patterns of each other's lives.
We are not shy now to complain
about aching joints or bad hips.
We are not above dying our hair pink
or dancing like we were twenty again.

It is time we claimed autumn for what it is—
obscenely colorful, its fierce blue skies,
red apples and sun unleash wild prayers.
There is still time, they whisper,
to greet the holiness of each new day.
Still time to put on our party shoes.

From where I sit by the kitchen window,
memories merge, drop like falling leaves
into the ground of me. In the dusky evening,
the photograph begins to shimmer until
the years dissolve, and it is only the threads
holding us together that still shine.
There is still time, there is still time.

Returning

They bought the house in late August
just as the light began to fade,
as tomatoes still on the vine
surrendered their sweetness,
as goldenrod scorched meadows,
as fires were kindled
to warm chilly mornings.
They moved in early November,
well aware that this far north
this time of year, light ebbs
flowing back into a sea of darkness,
compressing days into no more
than knobs that open drawers
full of night and stars.
By December they were settled back
into this village on the coast of Maine
as if they'd never left,
trusting the light would return
just as they had,
in time to grab the brass ring,
a chance to live a radiant life.

After 60

The construction worker who used
to whistle looks away,
the librarian offers to help you
find a book,
the doctor asks if there are nonslip
pads for your throw rugs,
the bank teller asks to count
your money for you,
the young boy averts his eyes,
the young girl smiles warily
before running off.
Going eye to eye with age
is something to be avoided.

Only I want to tell them all
how relieved I am to have reached
this age, to not have to worry
if my hair is brushed or
there is mud on my shoes
that may or may not
match my dress,
or that my scarf is crooked.
I don't need anyone's approval
to lie in the warm grass,
for yet another August night,
to count falling stars
with my granddaughter
who can get all the way
to ten before, like the stars,
she descends into sleep.

Acknowledgments

Grateful acknowledgement goes to the editors of the following publications where all of these poems were first published.

Poets Nook
Muleskinner Journal
The Navigator
Balancing Act 2 Anthology
Goose River Anthology
The New York Quarterly
Writer's Almanac April Prize
*The Mercy of Light (*Finishing Line Press)
NPR *"Poems From Here"*
Sol Invictus
Maine Farms: A Journal of Maine Farmland Trust
Gravida

I am beyond grateful to Wild Rising Press. To Judyth Hill for her careful and gracious reading of these poems and to Mary Meade for her inspired and beautiful design work. I'm deeply appreciative of their support and inspiration. It's been a joy to work with them.

Thank you, Wimby Hoyt for allowing me to use your gorgeous painting. Maybe it was meant to be that after 60 plus years of friendship, your images and my words have finally met each other.

And grateful as well to my friends Anne Damrosch, Kim Ridley, and the late Jean Balderston for their support and careful reading of everything I send them and their always helpful suggestions. To my children, Alexander and Sara, thank you forever and always for believing in me. Thank you to my wonderful husband, Robert, whose engineer's mind and poetic heart never fail to take me to the edge and back again.

Author's Biography

Emily Blair Stribling is the author of *The Mercy of Light,* Finishing Line Press. Her work has appeared in several journals and reviews, and is included in *Goose River* and *Balancing Act 2* anthologies. She is the recipient of an American Book Award, New York City's Pen and Brush Award and a winner of *The Writer's Almanac* April Poetry Contest. Emily Blair Stribling is a poet, Episcopal priest, wife, mother and grandmother; she was born in the south but has made Brooklin, Maine, her beloved home for many years.

For this rich and delicate collection of poems, steeped in luminous memories of home, place, and beloveds and what remains memorable over time... the old-style serif typeface Sabon is perfect. Designed by the German-born typographer and designer Jan Tschichold for a group of German printers who sought a "harmonized" or uniform font that would look the same whether set by hand or on a Monotype or Linotype typesetting machine and released in 1967, this font is based on types created by none other than the renowned Claude Garamond and named after Jacques Sabon, a Frenchman who, four hundred years before, had bought some of Garamond's typefaces and moved to Frankfurt, bringing Garamond's iconic type into use in German printing. Garamond's classic types produce organic-shaped letters, resembling handwriting with a pen. Sabon LT Pro, Roman, like the best of Garmond-influenced types is elegant, with balanced, well-defined strokes. Emily Blair Stribling's poetry celebrates what remains constant even through loss and time, and Sabon celebrates the enduring legacy of Garamond's contribution to type. The titles in *Honeyed Light* are set in Avenir font, a sans-serif typeface designed in 1988 by Adrian Frutiger, another noted designer of typefaces, and released by Linotype GmbH. Intended to be a humanist counterpart to the geometric sans-serifs popular at the time, subtle, curvy, and unique—*avenir*, which is French for "future," is a nuanced and—again—harmonious type. And, like *Honeyed Light*, while the body text, Sabon, looks generously backward, Avenir looks quietly, beautifully, forward.